MALALA

Fiona Beddall

LEVEL 1

SCHOLASTIC

Written by: Fiona Beddall

Publisher: Jacquie Bloese

Development Editor: Sarah Silver

Designer: Mo Choy

Picture research: Pupak Navabpour

Photo credits:
Cover: S. Honda/Getty Images.
Pages 4 & 5: A. Burton, O. Scarff, AFP/Getty Images; A. Weston/Alamy; A. Niedringhaus/PA Photos; P. Hermes Furian/iStockphoto.
Pages 6–8: A. Qureshi, Anadolu, V. deViguerie/Getty Images.
Pages 10–12: J. Demarthon, AFP, A. Majeed/Getty Images.
Pages 14–17: A. Qureshi, J. Moore, V. deViguerie/Getty Images.
Pages 18–21: A. Qureshi, A. Majeed/AFP/Getty Images; PID/EPA/Camerapress.
Pages 24–29: PGP/Rex Features; Queen Elizabeth Hospital, R. Tabassum/AFP/ Getty Images; Caters News.
Pages 30–33: AFP, S. Honda, N. Waldron/Getty Images.
Pages 34 & 35: S. Marai/AFP/Getty Images; M. Ismael/Reuters; European Commision; www.letgirlslead.org/poder

Published by Scholastic Ltd. 2015

Mary Glasgow Magazines (Scholastic Ltd.)
Euston House
24 Eversholt Street
London NW1 1DB

Printed in Malaysia

Reprinted in 2016 and 2017.

Contents

MALALA

MALALA YOUSAFZAI is from Pakistan. In October 2012, the Taliban shot her on her school bus because she is a campaigner for girls' education.

MALALA'S FAMILY live with her in Britain.

Malala's father, **ZIAUDDIN**, is also a campaigner for girls' education. In Pakistan, he owned a group of schools.

Malala's mother, **TOR PEKAI**, didn't have much education as a child. Now she is learning to read, write, and speak English.

Her brother, **ATAL**, is seven years younger than her.

Her brother, **KUSHAL**, is two years younger than her.

THE PAKISTANI TALIBAN is an Islamic political group. Its leaders want to lead Pakistan. It does not believe in education for girls.

MAULANA FAZLULLAH was the leader of an Islamic political group, the TNSM. He is now an important man in the Pakistani Taliban.

PLACES

PAKISTAN

This is **Swat Valley** in Pakistan. Before the war there, a lot of Pakistanis liked going to this beautiful place for their holidays.

Malala lived in **Mingora**, a city in Swat Valley, before she moved to Britain.

Islamabad is one of Pakistan's biggest cities. The country's most important politicians live and work here.

Queen Elizabeth Hospital, Birmingham
The doctors at this hospital in the British city of Birmingham saved Malala's life.

Kushal School is a school for girls in Mingora. Malala's father, Ziauddin, owns the school, and Malala went here for many years.

MALALA

It was October the 9th, 2012. Fifteen-year-old Malala walked out of her school in Mingora, Pakistan, and onto the bus. As it drove her home through the busy streets of the city, she talked with the other girls on the bus about the test at school that day. Then they started singing a song.

When they were about five minutes from Malala's home, the driver stopped. There were two men with guns in front of the bus. They had long white clothes. They were Taliban!

The men walked onto the bus and shouted, 'Who is Malala?'

The girls said nothing, but some gave Malala a frightened look. That was enough for the men.

One of them walked close to Malala and shot her in the head.

Chapter 1
A Girl in Swat Valley

When Tor Pekai Yousafzai had her first child, her friends were sad for her. The child was a girl. It was 1997 and Tor Pekai lived with her husband Ziauddin in Mingora, the biggest city in Pakistan's beautiful Swat Valley. When there's a new little boy in Swat Valley, the father asks friends and family to a big lunch. People give the baby clothes and money. But when a little girl arrives, the father doesn't tell anyone. It's a sad day for the family.

Luckily for Malala, her father was different from other men in Swat Valley. He was very happy with his daughter. A son, Kushal, arrived two years later, and a second son, Atal, five years after that. But her father always loved talking to Malala and teaching her things.

Children playing on the streets in Mingora

A lot of girls in Pakistan didn't go to school.

'They're going to cook and clean for their husband when they're older,' said their fathers. 'They don't need an education.'

Malala's mother, Tor Pekai, never learned to read or write as a child. But Ziauddin wanted more for his daughter, Malala, and for the other girls in Mingora. He was the owner of a school, and girls' education was very important to him.

Malala enjoyed her lessons at her father's school, and playing games in the street with her brothers and friends. When she was eight, the family had enough money to buy a TV. Malala loved it, but she and her brother Kushal always wanted to watch different things.

There were often a lot of people at their home: people from the other houses in the street, friends of her father, and family. Her mother's and father's brothers and sisters often came to stay there with their children, sometimes for days, sometimes for months.

The women were usually at the back of the house. While they cooked, they talked about clothes, food and friends. In town, they always had a *hijab* over their head, or were in a *burqa*.

Hijabs and *burqas* are an important part of life for women in Pakistan. It isn't possible to go out without one.

A woman wearing a burqa (left) and a hijab (right).

At the front of the house, the men had tea and talked about politics. Malala liked taking tea to the men and listening to them. She loved hearing about the world away from Swat Valley.

EARTHQUAKE HITS SWAT VALLEY

There were often earthquakes in Pakistan, but the one in October 2005 was worse than all the others. Nothing terrible happened in Mingora, but in other places in and around Swat Valley, 75,000 people died. Many more people had no homes or food after the earthquake. They waited for help from their leaders in Islamabad, or from the American army not far away in Afghanistan. But for a long time, only one group was there to help: a political group called the TNSM.

The TNSM opened roads and helped to build houses. There were TNSM doctors. Other TNSM people gave food to hungry families and homes to children without mothers or fathers. They did a lot of good work.

But the TNSM was an Islamic* political group, and its people weren't only there to help.

'This earthquake came from God,' they said. 'He is angry with us. We need more Islamic laws in Pakistan, or something much worse is going to happen.'

People were very frightened after the earthquake, and many of them believed the TNSM. It was the start of a terrible time for Swat Valley.

* Islamic laws and ideas come from the teaching of Mohammad and the Quran (the book of Islam).

CHAPTER 2
THE LAWS OF GOD

A few months after the earthquake, an Islamic lawyer came to Malala's home with six other men. 'Your school for girls is against the laws of God,' he said to Malala's father, Ziauddin. 'You must close it.'

Ziauddin often read the Quran with his family and tried to follow the teaching of Mohammad. He didn't believe that there was anything in this great book against girls' education.

Malala's father, Ziauddin Yousafzai

He and the Islamic lawyer talked and talked. After a long time, the lawyer decided that the biggest problem with the girls' school was the door. Girls went into the school through the same door as men.

'From tomorrow, the girls can use a different door,' said Ziauddin, and the school stayed open ... for now.

One day, after school, Malala heard a man on the radio. 'Don't smoke,' he said. 'Don't listen to music. Don't dance or watch films. God doesn't like these things.' The man started crying. 'Please live a good life, or there are going to be more earthquakes.'

Malala knew from school that earthquakes didn't happen because of smoking or music. But many people believed the man on the radio. When he cried, they cried too.

His name was Maulana Fazlullah and he was in the TNSM. He talked on the radio every evening, each time with more listeners. People liked his ideas.

'Our political leaders in Islamabad only want to be rich,' they said. 'They don't care about good laws. Maybe the laws of God are better for Pakistan.'

Maulana Fazlullah

But Fazlullah wanted a lot of changes. 'Women can only go out of the house when a man from their family is with them,' he said. 'And girls mustn't go to school.'

If someone said something against Fazlullah, Fazlullah soon knew about it. Then everyone heard that man's name on the radio.

'He doesn't care about the laws of God,' said Fazlullah. 'Is he going to be happy when more earthquakes come?'

Fazlullah asked people for money and bought guns for his men. The TNSM was now part of the Pakistani Taliban, and it was stronger every month. Soon there were no women in the centre of Mingora, and all the music and DVD shops in town closed. Fazlullah didn't like TVs, and his men listened for them in people's homes. Malala and her brothers still watched their favourite things, but with almost no sound.

Malala's school stayed open, but every month there were fewer girls. If a girl decided to leave school, Fazlullah named her on the radio.

'This girl's father is doing the right thing,' he said. 'But God is not happy with the girls still at school.'

Girls at a school in Mingora

DEAD BODIES IN MINGORA

Fazlullah's gunmen often took men from their homes at night. Family and friends found a dead body the next morning, and the words: 'This man died because he didn't follow God's laws.'

Ziauddin decided to talk to politicians in Islamabad about the problems with the Taliban in Swat Valley. He knew that it wasn't safe. But it was important to do something against Fazlullah.

After that, Ziauddin was often out in the evenings with other campaigners. When the Taliban followed him, he didn't come home. He didn't want to lead Fazlullah's men to his family.

'Are we going to find his dead body tomorrow?' thought Malala in her bed as she tried to sleep.

CHAPTER 3
A BBC BLOGGER

'We are at war with the politicians in Islamabad,' said the Taliban. But for a long time their only war was against campaigners like Ziauddin.

'Maybe the politicians don't care that the Taliban make the laws in Swat,' people thought.

But when Malala was ten, the Pakistani Army arrived in Mingora.

'They are here to save us from the Taliban!' Malala and her friends said happily.

The Pakistani army flying over Mingora

Soon there were no Taliban in the streets of Mingora. But they weren't far away, and they still had guns, men and money. At night, the army shot at the Taliban and the Taliban shot at the army. Everyone in Mingora was frightened. Malala and her brothers often went into their mother and father's bed, but sleep was difficult.

The war didn't stop for more than a year. But Ziauddin's three schools – one for younger children, one for older boys and a third for older girls – stayed open. Malala was now at the school for older girls, and she loved all her lessons. She hoped to be a doctor after she left school. Men did most of the important jobs in Pakistan, but the country needed women doctors. It wasn't possible for men doctors to care for women.

When school finished for the day, children didn't play in the streets. The streets weren't safe. And life was boring at home, because Fazlullah's men stopped everything on TV. There was only Fazlullah's radio show … and the bombs.

A school in the Swat Valley bombed by the Taliban

The Taliban bombed shops, roads and houses. They also bombed more than 200 schools – at night, when no one was there. But for Fazlullah, that wasn't enough. At the end of 2008, the Taliban said, 'From January the 15th, there are going to be no girls at school. Follow this law, or your girls are going to die.'

The army was still in Mingora. But it was impossible to keep every schoolgirl safe from the Taliban. In a few days, Malala's class went from twenty-seven girls to eleven. Those eleven girls waited sadly for January the 15th and the end of their education.

SWAT SCHOOLGIRL WRITES BLOG FOR BBC

Ziauddin and his friends campaigned against this new law. They talked to politicians in Islamabad and to reporters from other countries. Luckily, the BBC* wanted to help. For its website in Urdu, Pakistan's most important language, it wanted the blog of a Swat Valley schoolgirl. This was a great way to tell the world about the problems in Swat. Ziauddin looked for a writer, but schoolgirls were frightened. They all said no.

'I can write it,' said Malala.

Ziauddin and Tor Pekai agreed. 'But don't put your name on the blog,' they said.

Malala's blog started on January the 3rd. She wrote about her bad dreams about the Taliban. Then she wrote about her walk home from school that day, when a man

* The BBC makes TV and radio in Britain, and has websites in a lot of different languages.

behind her said, 'You're dead.' She was frightened, and walked faster and faster. Then she turned and looked at the man. He had a mobile phone in his hand. His words weren't for Malala – they were for someone on the phone.

At school everyone loved the blog, and they wanted to know the blogger's name. Malala said nothing.

Ziauddin talked to lots of reporters about the problems in Swat, and sometimes Malala came with him. On the morning before Fazlullah's law started, an American TV reporter arrived at their house. He wanted to film Malala's last day at school. Ziauddin wasn't happy about this at first, but in the end he agreed.

Before she went to school, maybe for the last time, Malala talked to the camera. 'They can't stop me. I'm going to have an education, if it's at home, or school, or any place.'

They were strong words, but she didn't feel very strong. As she thought about life without her lessons, her teachers and her schoolfriends, she started to cry.

Malala at her home in Mingora

CHAPTER 4
WITHOUT A HOME

In the days after her school closed, Malala wrote more of her blog. It was now on English websites as well as the Urdu one, and in a Pakistani newspaper too.

Sometimes Malala read her schoolbooks alone in her room, but it wasn't much fun without her friends. She was very happy when, after six weeks away from school, the Taliban and the Pakistan army agreed to end the war. Girls' education was part of the peace agreement, and girls' schools opened again.

MILLIONS LEAVE THEIR HOMES IN SWAT

But people quickly started breaking the agreement, and in May the war started again. This time, Tor Pekai didn't want to stay in Mingora. She decided to take Malala and the boys to her family home in the country.

People leaving their homes in Mingora

More than two million people left their homes. Some were in cars, with big bags of clothes and food. Others were on bikes or on foot. It usually took a few hours to drive from Mingora to Tor Pekai's family, but that time it took two days. They walked the last twenty-four kilometres with all their bags on their backs.

Ziauddin didn't come with them to Tor Pekai's family. He lived and worked with other campaigners in the city of Peshawar. The work was important, but it was difficult for the children without their father. When Malala turned twelve, he forgot her birthday. She was very angry with him.

After three months, the war ended and the people of Swat Valley went home. As Malala saw Mingora again, she thought about all her country's problems, and her plans to be a doctor. Pakistan already had a lot of good doctors, but it needed better political leaders. She decided to be a politician.

The Taliban didn't make the laws in Swat now but they still bombed schools. And they bombed one of Ziauddin's campaigner friends and shot another. They wanted Ziauddin dead too. They also knew Malala's face from the American film.

'But that's OK,' thought her mother and father. 'The Taliban kill men, but they never kill children.'

When Malala didn't think about the Taliban, life was good. She talked a lot on TV about girls' education. She was also in a new political group for children. Every month, young people from different parts of Swat Valley came together and decided on the biggest problems for children. Malala, as the group's leader, then asked the politicians of Swat for change.

'Street children must have more help with their

education,' the group said. 'And after all the Taliban bombs, we need lots of new school buildings.'

The politicians of Swat listened to the group's ideas, and sometimes changes happened. It was exciting to make a difference.

PAKISTAN PEACE PRIZE FOR MALALA

It was exciting, too, when people remembered Malala's hard work. When she was fourteen, a friend ran into class one day. 'You've got a prize, Malala!' There were lots of reporters at the school, and they all wanted to talk to her.

A few weeks later, Malala went to Islamabad and a famous politician gave her the prize. It was Pakistan's first Young Person's Peace Prize. Every year after that, there was a peace prize for a young Pakistani. Its name was the Malala Prize.

The Young Person's Peace Prize, 2011

CHAPTER 5
'WE CAN'T STOP NOW'

'Malala Yousafzai must die.' Malala and her family read the Taliban's words on the Internet. But Malala wasn't the same girl as three years ago, when she was frightened of a man on a mobile phone. Her father wanted to stop the campaign and keep her safe. But she didn't agree.

'Some things are more important than our lives,' she told him. 'We can't stop now.'

* * *

Malala wanted to be a politician in Islamabad one day and give everyone in Pakistan a better education. But before that happened, she wanted to do useful things in Swat. Mingora's poorest children worked all day in difficult jobs, and many of them lived on the streets. When she was fifteen, Malala decided to help them. She talked to her schoolfriends about these children's problems, and together they started a charity.

Children working in Mingora

Malala's father still campaigned against the Taliban, but he was frightened for Malala. A lot of his campaigner friends were dead now. Who was next? Every night, he came into Malala's room to close the windows. 'Now the Taliban can't come in. You're safe!' he said. But Malala didn't feel safe. She often had bad dreams.

Soon it was time for the school tests. Malala liked to be top of the class, but the year before, because of all her campaign work, she only came second.

Her brother Kushal laughed. 'You're the most famous schoolgirl in Pakistan,' he said, 'but you're not the cleverest!'

This year Malala wanted to be top again. She read her schoolbooks for hours before each test.

* * *

October the 9th was an exciting day for Tor Pekai. In the afternoon, she planned to have her first reading and writing lesson. Malala said goodbye to her after a quick breakfast, and got on the bus to school. Her test went well. She was very happy as she talked to her friends on the way home.

Malala can't remember anything else from that day. She can't remember the Taliban on the bus, or their question, 'Who is Malala?' She can't remember the gun at her head. And she can't remember the moment when the man started shooting.

Chapter 6
BIRMINGHAM

Seven days later, Malala started to wake up. She saw some people, but who were they? And where was she? She tried to ask. But no sound came from her mouth.

Soon she saw that she was in a hospital. So why weren't her mother and father there with her? She was very frightened. Were they dead?

A doctor talked to her in Urdu. 'I brought you here from Pakistan,' he said. 'You are safe now.'

She wanted to ask questions. But that wasn't possible because there was a tube through her nose and the back of her mouth. Someone gave her a pen and paper. She wrote 'father', and then 'country'.

'You are in Birmingham,' said the doctor, Dr* Javid.

But Malala didn't know that Birmingham was in Britain. And why didn't the doctor say anything about her father? 'Something terrible happened to my family,' she thought. 'And the doctors are only going to tell me when I'm stronger.'

The next day she met a different doctor, Dr Fiona. 'Your father is safe,' the doctor told her. 'He's in Pakistan.' She gave her a picture of him from yesterday's newspaper. Her mother and her brother Atal were there at the back of the photo too. Malala started to feel better.

The day after that, one of the doctors said, 'We're going to phone your mother and father. But don't cry. Be strong for them.'

'Malala? Is that you?' said her father on the other end of the phone. She said nothing because of the tube in the back of her mouth, but she was so happy to hear him again.

* Dr is short for Doctor.

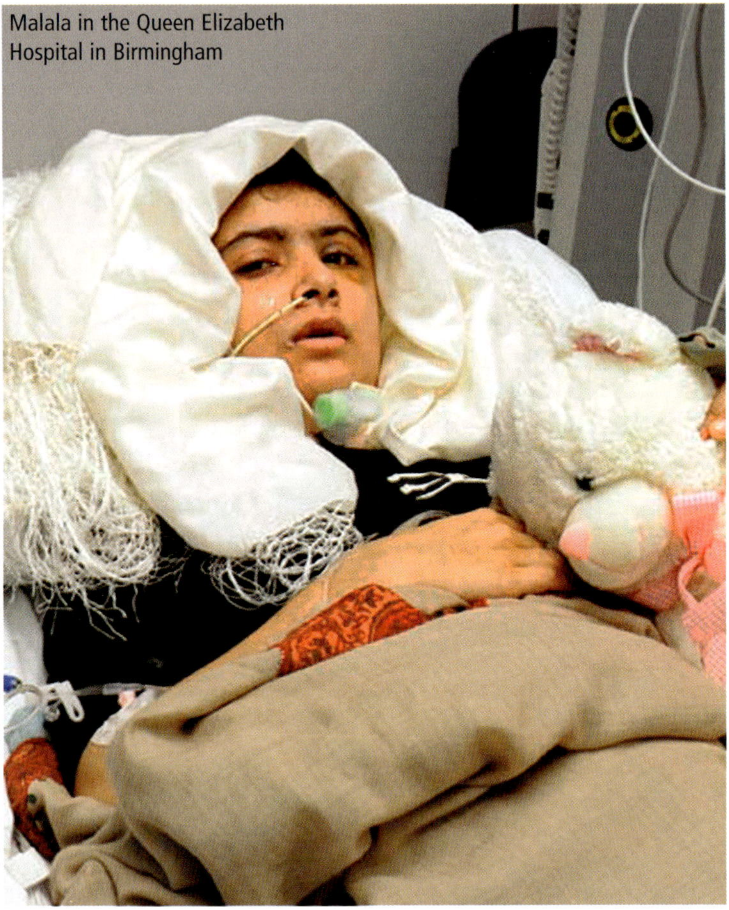

Malala in the Queen Elizabeth Hospital in Birmingham

One day, Malala saw her face. It was blue and yellow around her left eye, and she had no hair on part of her head. The left of her mouth went down in a funny way. It wasn't pretty, but she didn't cry. She only wanted to understand.

'Who did this to me?' she wrote. 'Did someone shoot me?'

'Yes,' said Dr Fiona sadly. 'On the bus, on your way

home from school. He shot two other girls too, Shazia and Kainat. They're in hospital in Pakistan, but they're going to be OK.'

Shazia and Kainat were Malala's friends, but she didn't remember them. She didn't remember a lot of things.

Later, she learned more. After the gunman shot her, the bus driver took her to Mingora Hospital. She went to two other hospitals – the first in Peshawar, the other near Islamabad – and almost died. The doctors saved her life. But after that, she needed months of care in a safer country. Two of her doctors in Pakistan, Dr Fiona and Dr Javid, were from Britain. They took her to Dr Javid's hospital, the Queen Elizabeth Hospital in Birmingham.

But there was a problem for the family. Only Ziauddin had the right papers to leave Pakistan. He wanted to go with Malala to Birmingham, but Tor Pekai and the boys had no friends near Islamabad. He didn't want to leave them alone. Ziauddin and Tor Pekai decided to go to Britain together in two or three days, when they all had papers. But the papers didn't come. They waited and waited.

CHAPTER 7
TOGETHER AGAIN

After five days in Birmingham, the doctors took the tube out of Malala's nose. It was possible to speak again! She talked to her family on the phone … but still they didn't come to Britain.

After another five days Dr Javid had some good news. 'Your family is coming today,' he said.

But Malala didn't believe him. She always hoped to see them. But they never came.

A few hours later, she heard people behind the door. The door opened, and four people ran to her. Her family had their papers and they were here!

For the first time in hospital, she cried. And she didn't stop. She cried and cried and cried.

Malala with her family in hospital

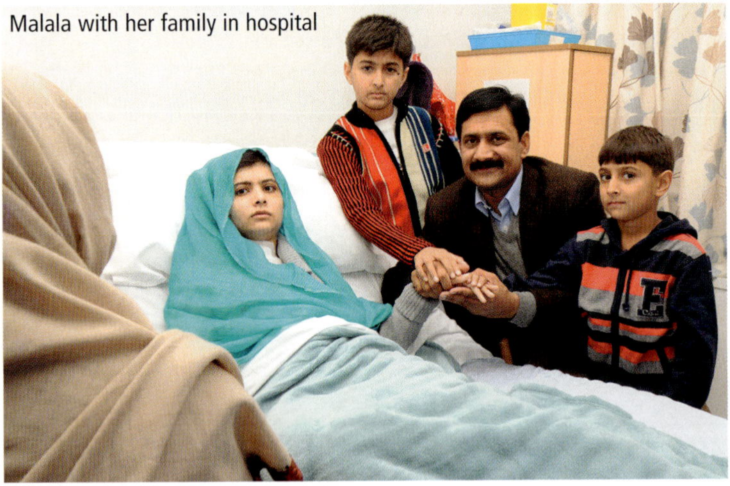

After the shooting, Malala's left eye didn't close, and her mouth didn't smile. But the doctors worked hard on those problems, and slowly she learned to smile again.

She remembered more words, too, and more things about her life. And she learned to walk again. It was very difficult at first, but every week it was easier.

One day someone from the hospital gave her a big bag of letters. 'Fantastic! They're from my friends!' she thought. But they weren't from her friends in Pakistan. They were from people all over the world. This bag was one of many. In all, she had more than eight thousand letters!

Malala learned that her shooting was in hundreds of newspapers. And lots of famous people talked about it – from Barack Obama to Selena Gomez*. People in Pakistan and many other countries campaigned against the shooting. Reporters called her the world's most famous teenager.

Children in Pakistan campaigning against the shooting

Malala thought about all those days alone in her hospital bedroom. But she wasn't alone. She had the love of hundreds of thousands of people. The Taliban shot

* Selena Gomez is a famous American singer.

her because they wanted to stop her campaign for girls' education. But now, because of the shooting, thousands more people wanted to help the campaign.

Malala leaving hospital

After three months in hospital, Malala went to live with her family in Birmingham. Her father had a good job in the city, and they had a nice house. Ziauddin helped around the house more than in Pakistan, and Tor Pekai worked hard at her reading, writing and English. But their life at home was very quiet and very boring. There were no friends or family in the kitchen. There were no children's games in the street. And every house looked the same.

In the city centre, it was more exciting – and very different from Pakistan! Men and women in cafés talked together as friends. And how did the girls stay warm in their little skirts and short tops in the cold Birmingham weather?

When she was stronger, Malala started going to school. The new school had a lot of fantastic things: computers, videos, art lessons. But it didn't have the most important thing from her old school: her friends. Malala sometimes talked to her Mingora friends on the Internet, and the girls at the new school were kind. But in Birmingham, she was always someone famous, someone different. She wanted to be 'just Malala' again.

Malala on her first day at school in Birmingham

CHAPTER 8
TAKING THE CAMPAIGN TO THE WORLD

Malala didn't have much time to think about friends. There was a lot to do when she wasn't at school.

When she was in hospital, a group of people from around the world started a new charity, the Malala Fund. Now they wanted Malala to lead the charity.

Malala in Zaatari, Jordan

Malala went to Zaatari in Jordan. 60,000 Syrian children were there because of a war in Syria, but there were only three schools for them all. The Malala Fund helped to give them an education. In Kenya, Malala helped to build an all-girls school. And in Nigeria, she campaigned against an Islamic group, Boko Haram, after it took more than two hundred girls from their school. Malala wanted more help from the President of Nigeria to find the girls.

Malala Talks To United Nations

The United Nations decided to call her birthday, July the 12th, Malala Day. On the first Malala Day, nine months after the shooting on the bus, she talked to a big group of politicians and young campaigners at the United Nations. She talked of peace and love, and of children's problems in different countries.

'One child, one teacher, one book and one pen can change the world,' she said.

Malala speaking at the United Nations

NOBEL PRIZE FOR MALALA

The next year, there was a very exciting email. 'You've got the 2014 Nobel Peace Prize,' it said. The prize was for both Malala and an Indian campaigner for children, Kailash Satyarthi. Malala was only seventeen – the world's youngest person with a Nobel Prize.

'You see only one girl in front of you,' said Malala when she went to Norway for her prize. 'But I am not one girl ... I am 66 million girls without an education. And today, I am not talking. Those 66 million girls are talking.

'We children don't understand our leaders. Why can the "strong" countries of the world easily bring war, but not peace? Why can they give guns, but not books? Why can they build bombs, but not schools?'

* * *

Most people in Pakistan were very angry about Malala's shooting. But when Malala and a British reporter wrote a book about her life, many Pakistanis didn't like it.

'She thinks like an American, not a Pakistani,' said reporters.

'She isn't a good Muslim,' said leaders of Pakistani schools. 'Our children mustn't read her book.'

Malala hopes to live back in Pakistan one day, but at the moment it isn't safe. The police found the gunmen from the bus after two years, but they didn't find the men's leader, Fazlullah. In December 2014, 141 children and teachers died when Taliban gunmen went into a school in

Peshawar. Many people think that those shootings were Fazlullah's idea. And Fazlullah still wants Malala dead.

Malala hopes to be a politician, and maybe one day the political leader of Pakistan. She wants to bring peace to her country. As she said when she heard about her Nobel Prize, 'This is not the end of my campaign. This is only the start.'

GIRLS FOR

Malala isn't the only teenager with big ideas for change. Meet these fantastic girls from around the world.

CYCLING FOR FREEDOM

Most girls in Afghanistan can't choose their own husbands. They can't wear short skirts or drive cars. And bikes are only for boys. But a group of Afghan women want to change that. They are in the first Afghan Women's Cycling Team. Men often shout angrily when they see them on a bike. But when women see them, some want to cycle too. The team thinks that cycling can bring other changes for women in their country.

The Afghan Women's Cycling Team near Kabul

A RUBBISH IDEA

Azza Abdel Hamid Faiad is from Alexandria, Cairo. There's a lot of plastic rubbish in her city. It's a big problem. But when she was sixteen, Azza found a way to make biofuel from this old plastic. 'It's safe and it's cheap,' she said. 'And with all the plastic rubbish from Egypt in one year, we can make $78 million of biofuel.' People are hoping to use Azza's biofuel in cars very soon.

Azza Faiad

CHANGE

CHANGE IN GUATEMALA

When Emelin Cabrera and Elba Velasquez talked about their schoolwork, the boys always laughed. 'Why do you come to school? Girls are only useful when they have children!' Emelin and Elba wanted a better life for the girls in their town in Guatemala. They wrote a report about the small number of girls in school and the high number of teenage mothers. Now girls in the town can see a doctor more easily. And more girls can have a good education.

Emelin and Elba

What changes do you want for your country or the world? How can you help to make those changes?

What do these words mean? You can use a dictionary.

cycle freedom plastic rubbish biofuel

CHAPTERS 1–2

Before you read

You can use your dictionary.

1 Complete the sentences with these words.

agree campaign God leader politics save shoot

a) We are starting a … for better food at our school.
b) I work in … because I want changes in our country.
c) Please don't … me! I can't help you if I'm dead!
d) She and I have opposite ideas about everything. We never … .
e) He's going to die. Nothing can … him now.
f) Long ago in Egypt, people believed in Ra, the … of the Sun.
g) Barack Obama became the … of the USA in 2009.

2 Match the two halves of these sentences.

a) People go to school because they want	**i)** a gun.
b) When two countries fight, there's	**ii)** an earthquake.
c) Three or more people together are	**iii)** a group.
d) To shoot someone, you need	**iv)** an education.
e) Buildings sometimes fall down in	**v)** a war.

3 Read 'People and Places' on pages 4–5 and answer the questions.

a) Where are Malala and her family from?
b) How many brothers and sisters does Malala have?
c) Where do Malala and her family live now?

After you read

4 Complete the sentences with the correct names.

a) … didn't learn to read and write as a child.
b) The … helped a lot of people after an earthquake.
c) A lot of people listened to …'s ideas on the radio.

5 True or false? Correct the false sentences.

a) Malala was with her family when the Taliban shot her.
b) Women in Swat Valley always wear a *hijab* or *burqa* in town.
c) When people gave Fazlullah money, he bought school books.
d) Music and DVD shops closed because of the earthquake.

Chapters 3–4

Before you read

You can use your dictionary.

6 Complete the sentences with these words.

army bomb peace prize reporter

a) I want to be a … for a newspaper.
b) I don't want to be in the … because I don't want to go to war.
c) There's a £100 … for the best picture.
d) There are too many wars in the world. Why can't we have …?
e) There was a ... in the city yesterday and thirty people died.

7 Chapter 4 is called 'Without a Home'. Who is going to be without a home, do you think? Why?

After you read

8 When did these things happen? Number them 1–7.

a) Malala joined a new political group for children.
b) Fazlullah said, 'From January the 15th, there are going to be no girls at school.'
c) Malala started writing a blog.
d) The war started again, and lots of people left Mingora.
e) Malala's school closed.
f) The Pakistani army arrived in Mingora and war started.
g) Malala and her family came back to Mingora and she decided to be a politician.

9 Answer the questions.

a) Why did Malala want to be a doctor?
b) Where did people read Malala's blog?
c) Where did Malala go when the war started again?
d) Why was she angry with her father on her birthday?
e) Why were there reporters at Malala's school in 2011?

10 What do you think? Was Malala right to write a blog and campaign on TV? Were her mother and father right to say yes to the idea?

CHAPTERS 5–6

Before you read

11 Answer the questions.

a) Do you help any *charities*? Which ones? How?

b) Where do you see *tubes*? What are they for?

12 In Chapter 6, Malala goes to Birmingham, England. Can you find it on a map? Why does she go there, do you think?

After you read

13 Who ...

a) wanted to stop Malala's campaign after the Taliban said 'Malala must die'?

b) laughed at Malala because she wasn't top of the class at school?

c) did the Taliban on the bus shoot, as well as Malala?

d) took Malala to Mingora Hospital?

e) took Malala from Pakistan to England?

14 Write these words in the sentences.

campaign charity dead face family friends hospital life papers shooting

a) Malala thought that her ... was more important than her ... .

b) Malala and her ... started a ... to help poor children.

c) In Birmingham, Malala was scared at first that her ... was ... .

d) Malala's ... was blue and yellow after the ... .

e) Her family weren't at the ... because her mother and brothers didn't have the right ... .

15 What do you think?

a) You are Malala. You read the Taliban's words, 'Malala must die'. Do you stop your campaign? Why / Why not?

b) You are Shazia and Kainat, the other girls in the shooting on the bus. Are you angry with Malala? Why / Why not?

c) You are Malala's father, Ziauddin. You can go with Malala to England but your family can't go with you. Do you stay with your family or go with Malala? Why?

Chapters 7–8

Before you read

16 What do you think?

a) What did Malala like or hate about Birmingham when she left hospital?

b) Did she go to school again? Where?

c) Did she go back to Pakistan? Why / Why not?

After you read

17 Are these sentences true or false? Correct the false sentences.

a) Malala cried when she saw her family in the hospital.

b) Because of the shooting, she can't smile now.

c) In hospital, she had a big bag of letters from her friends.

d) People in Pakistan were angry about the shooting.

e) In other countries, no one cared about the shooting.

f) Malala's mother had a good job in Birmingham.

g) Malala had better schoolfriends in Birmingham than in Mingora.

18 Choose the correct place for each sentence.

Jordan Nigeria Norway Pakistan Peshawar

a) There were a lot of children without schools, because of a war in Syria.

b) An Islamic group, Boko Haram, took 200 girls from their school.

c) Someone gave Malala her Nobel Peace Prize.

d) People said 'Our children mustn't read Malala's book.'

e) The Taliban shot lots of children and teachers in a school.

19 What do you think?

a) Can you name any other Nobel Peace Prize winners? What did they do to win their prize?

b) Malala said, 'One child, one teacher, one book and one pen can change the world.' Do you agree? Why / Why not?

c) Is Malala going to be a political leader in Pakistan one day? Can she change her country? Why / Why not?

NEW WORDS

What do these words mean?

agree (v) .... / agreement (n) ....

army (n) ....

bomb (n & v) ....

campaign (n) .... / campaigner (n) ....

charity (n) ....

earthquake (n) ....

education (n) ....

God (n) ....

group (n) ....

gun (n) ....

law (n) .... / lawyer (n) ....

lead (v) .... / leader (n) ....

peace (n) ....

politics (n) .... / politician (n) .... /
political (adj) ....

prize (n) ....

report (n) .... / reporter (n) ....

save (v) .... safe (adj) ....

shoot (v) *past* shot .... / shooting (n) ....

tube (n) ....

war (n) ....